DISCARD

STATE PROFILES

📍 SOUTH DAKOTA

BY BETSY RATHBURN

BLASTOFF! DISCOVERY

BELLWETHER MEDIA • MINNEAPOLIS, MN

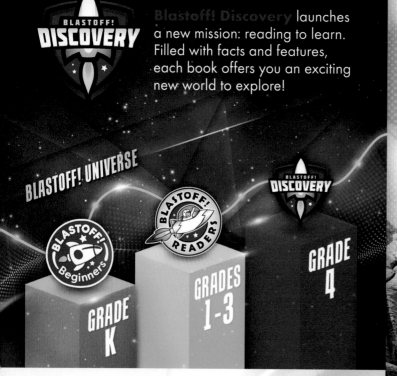

Blastoff! Discovery launches a new mission: reading to learn. Filled with facts and features, each book offers you an exciting new world to explore!

BLASTOFF! UNIVERSE

BLASTOFF! Beginners

BLASTOFF! READERS

BLASTOFF! DISCOVERY

GRADE K

GRADES 1-3

GRADE 4

This edition first published in 2022 by Bellwether Media, Inc.

No part of this publication may be reproduced in whole or in part without written permission of the publisher.
For information regarding permission, write to Bellwether Media, Inc., Attention: Permissions Department,
6012 Blue Circle Drive, Minnetonka, MN 55343.

Library of Congress Cataloging-in-Publication Data

Names: Rathburn, Betsy, author.
Title: South Dakota / by Betsy Rathburn.
Description: Minneapolis, MN : Bellwether Media, Inc., 2022. |
    Series: Blastoff! Discovery: State profiles | Includes bibliographical
    references and index. | Audience: Ages 7-13 |
    Audience: Grades 4-6 | Summary: "Engaging images accompany
    information about South Dakota. The combination of high-interest
    subject matter and narrative text is intended for students in grades
    3 through 8"– Provided by publisher.
Identifiers: LCCN 2021020848 (print) | LCCN 2021020849
    (ebook) | ISBN 9781644873472 (library binding) | ISBN
    9781648341908 (ebook)
Subjects: LCSH: South Dakota–Juvenile literature.
Classification: LCC F651.3 .R37 2022 (print) | LCC F651.3
    (ebook) | DDC 978.3–dc23
LC record available at https://lccn.loc.gov/2021020848
LC ebook record available at https://lccn.loc.gov/2021020849

Editor: Colleen Sexton   Designer: Andrea Schneider

Printed in the United States of America, North Mankato, MN.

TABLE OF CONTENTS

It has been a long day of hiking through Badlands National Park. A family pauses to take in the view. Jagged **pinnacles** and smooth mounds rise from the earth. The sun brightens red and brown stripes that formed in the rock over millions of years. An endless **prairie** stretches for miles in every direction.

BIG STONE LAKE

CUSTER STATE PARK

DEADWOOD

MOUNT RUSHMORE

WALL DRUG

Wall Drug sits just outside the Badlands. In the 1930s, this huge store became famous for its free ice water. Today, hundreds of Wall Drug signs along the highway draw visitors to the store.

The family has one more trail to explore. They follow the Fossil Exhibit Trail. On the trail, **replicas** of fossils stand where dinosaurs once roamed. South Dakota has so much to discover!

South Dakota is in the **Upper Midwest** region of the United States. This rectangle-shaped state covers 77,116 square miles (199,730 square kilometers). Its capital, Pierre, is in the center of the state. It sits on the banks of the Missouri River. Other major cities include Sioux Falls, Rapid City, and Aberdeen.

Minnesota and Iowa are South Dakota's eastern neighbors. Nebraska lies to the south. South Dakota shares its western border with Wyoming and Montana. North Dakota borders the state to the north.

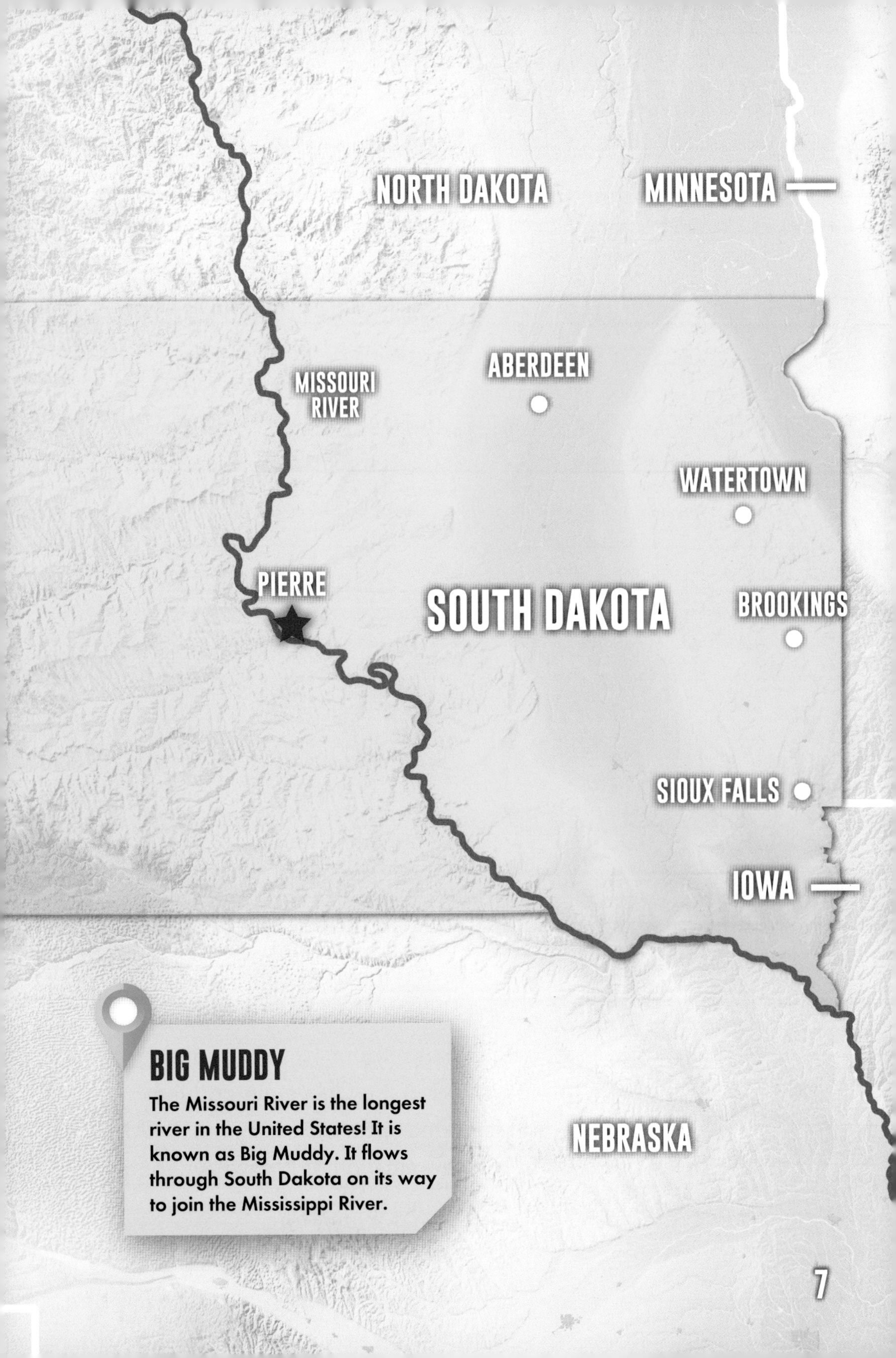

NORTH DAKOTA   MINNESOTA ─

ABERDEEN

MISSOURI
RIVER
                                           WATERTOWN

PIERRE   SOUTH DAKOTA   BROOKINGS

                                           SIOUX FALLS

                                           IOWA ─

BIG MUDDY

The Missouri River is the longest
river in the United States! It is
known as Big Muddy. It flows
through South Dakota on its way
to join the Mississippi River.

NEBRASKA

BISON CROSSING
THE GREAT PLAINS

People came to South Dakota about 10,000 years ago.
The first known groups included the Cheyenne and the
Arikara. They hunted bison and grew crops. By the 1700s,
the Sioux people had pushed most other Native American
groups out of South Dakota.

French-Canadians were the first white people to explore South Dakota. These fur trappers traded along the Missouri River. In 1803, the United States bought South Dakota as part of the **Louisiana Purchase**. But the Sioux fought the U.S. government to keep their land. The **Wounded Knee Massacre** in 1890 ended the Sioux people's efforts. South Dakota became a state in 1889.

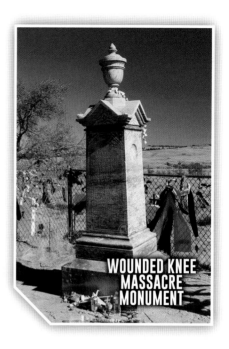

WOUNDED KNEE MASSACRE MONUMENT

NATIVE PEOPLES OF SOUTH DAKOTA

THE SIOUX NATION

- Original lands stretched from Minnesota to the Rocky Mountains
- More than 72,000 in South Dakota today
- Federally recognized tribes include the Cheyenne River Sioux, Crow Creek Sioux, Flandreau Santee Sioux, Lower Brule Sioux, Oglala Sioux, Rosebud Sioux, and Yankton Sioux
- The Standing Rock Sioux and Sisseton-Wahpeton Oyate tribes have lands in both South Dakota and North Dakota
- Also called Dakota, Lakota, and Nakota

Much of South Dakota is flat. Prairies and farmland make up the Central Lowlands in the east. This region reaches to the Missouri River, which flows north to south through the middle of the state. Dams on the river create **reservoirs**. The grasslands of the **Great Plains** spread across western South Dakota. The land rises to the peaks of the Black Hills in the southwest. Thick pine forests cover the rocky slopes.

LAKE OAHE

MISSOURI RIVER

GREAT PLAINS   CENTRAL LOWLANDS
BLACK HILLS

LAKE OAHE

LAKE OAHE

A dam on the Missouri River holds back water to create Lake Oahe. This reservoir is South Dakota's largest lake and the fourth-largest reservoir in the United States.

SPRING
HIGH: 57°F (14°C)
LOW: 33°F (1°C)

SUMMER
HIGH: 83°F (28°C)
LOW: 57°F (14°C)

FALL
HIGH: 59°F (15°C)
LOW: 34°F (1°C)

WINTER
HIGH: 30°F (-1°C)
LOW: 9°F (-13°C)

°F = degrees Fahrenheit
°C = degrees Celsius

BADLANDS
NATIONAL PARK

South Dakota is known for its cold, snowy winters.
Summers are hot with temperatures that can reach
115 degrees Fahrenheit (46 degrees Celsius)!
Powerful storms sometimes bring tornadoes.

South Dakota is full of wildlife! White-tailed deer wander in fields and forests. Northern leopard frogs hop near rivers and ponds. In the prairie, black-tailed prairie dogs build underground homes. They poke their heads out of holes to watch for coyotes and hawks. Prairie rattlesnakes lie in wait in the tall grass. Pheasants and greater prairie-chickens peck at the ground for insects.

Pronghorn roam the land just west of the Missouri River. Farther west, bighorn sheep climb rocky hills. Special parks give homes to American bison. South Dakota's bats find shelter in caves.

► SOUTH DAKOTA'S FUTURE: CLIMATE CHANGE

Climate change is affecting South Dakota's wildlife. Hotter, drier weather leads to more wildfires. More powerful storms cause flooding. These events may destroy areas where animals live.

NORTHERN LEOPARD FROG

PRAIRIE RATTLESNAKE

GREATER PRAIRIE-CHICKEN

PRONGHORN

BLACK-TAILED
PRAIRIE DOG

Life Span: up to 8 years
Status: least concern

black-tailed
prairie dog range =

LEAST CONCERN	NEAR THREATENED	VULNERABLE	ENDANGERED	CRITICALLY ENDANGERED	EXTINCT IN THE WILD	EXTINCT

13

About 886,000 people live in South Dakota. More than half of South Dakotans make their homes in **urban** areas. Nearly one out of every four live in Sioux Falls, the largest city. Some Native Americans live on the state's nine **reservations**.

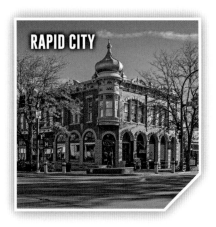

RAPID CITY

PINE RIDGE INDIAN RESERVATION

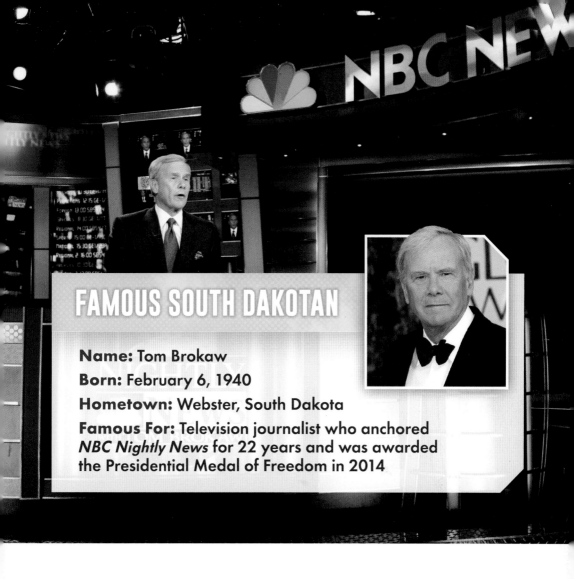

FAMOUS SOUTH DAKOTAN

Name: Tom Brokaw
Born: February 6, 1940
Hometown: Webster, South Dakota
Famous For: Television journalist who anchored *NBC Nightly News* for 22 years and was awarded the Presidential Medal of Freedom in 2014

Most South Dakotans have **ancestors** from Germany, Norway, Ireland, and other European countries. About 1 in 10 are Native American. Asian Americans, Hispanic Americans, and Black or African Americans make up a small part of the population. Some South Dakotans are **immigrants**. Newcomers have arrived from Guatemala, the Philippines, Mexico, Sudan, and Ethiopia.

Land **speculators** founded Sioux Falls on the Big Sioux River in 1856. **Settlers** faced cold winters and conflicts with Native Americans. Some years, grasshoppers ate their crops. But the town grew after the railroad arrived in 1878. Today, Sioux Falls is South Dakota's largest city and center of industry.

FALLS PARK

Falls Park is a popular place to visit in Sioux Falls. It is home to the Big Sioux River waterfalls that give Sioux Falls its name!

Many residents work or study at the city's universities. For outdoor fun, people head to the Big Sioux Recreation Area. Downtown shoppers enjoy the SculptureWalk's outdoor artworks. Residents also browse art galleries and science exhibits at Washington Pavilion. They can catch a play at the Orpheum Theater or an outdoor concert at Levitt at the Falls.

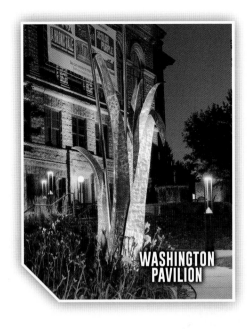

WASHINGTON PAVILION

SCULPTUREWALK

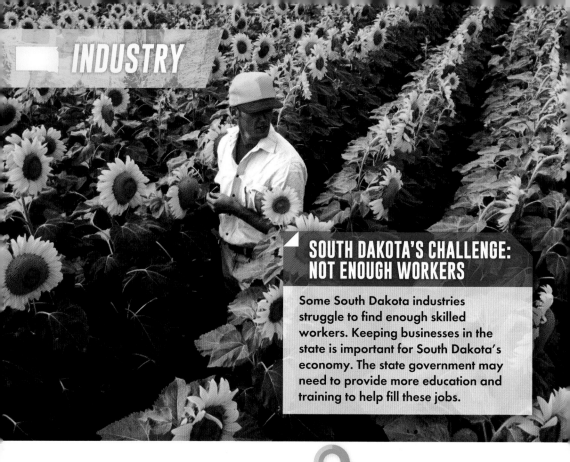

SOUTH DAKOTA'S CHALLENGE: NOT ENOUGH WORKERS

Some South Dakota industries struggle to find enough skilled workers. Keeping businesses in the state is important for South Dakota's economy. The state government may need to provide more education and training to help fill these jobs.

Farming was one of South Dakota's first industries. Today, soybeans, sunflowers, wheat, and hogs are among the most valuable farm products. Many factory workers process and pack those products. Others make machinery and computer parts. Loggers work in the forests of the Black Hills. They produce wood for sawmills and paper companies.

MOUNT RUSHMORE

Mount Rushmore is South Dakota's most popular tourist attraction. It shows the faces of U.S. presidents George Washington, Thomas Jefferson, Theodore Roosevelt, and Abraham Lincoln. Each face is about 60 feet (18 meters) high!

Miners also work in the Black Hills, where they dig up gold. Other mined products in South Dakota include oil, natural gas, sand, and gravel. Most South Dakotans have **service jobs**. They work in government offices, hospitals, and schools. **Tourism** also employs many service workers.

OIL DRILLING

INVENTED IN SOUTH DAKOTA

FIRST AMERICAN FOUR-DOOR CAR
Date Invented: 1908
Inventor: Thomas Fawick

MODERN HOT-AIR BALLOON SYSTEM
Date Invented: 1960
Inventor: Ed Yost

BIEROCKS

South Dakotans' favorite foods reflect their backgrounds. Germans brought *bierocks*. Meat and cabbage fill these doughy buns. **Fry bread** became common on reservations in the 1800s. Native Americans first made it out of limited baking supplies. Today, Native American cooks often serve it at **powwows**.

Many South Dakotans enjoy chislic. Cubed meat is seasoned, grilled, and served on skewers. Hunters bring pheasant, **venison**, and other wild game to the table. Walleye dinners appear on many menus. For dessert, bakers make sweet, fruit-filled pastries called kolaches. *Kuchen* is another favorite treat. Fruit and custard fill this **traditional** German cake.

WALLEYE

KOLACHES

APPLE CREAM CHEESE KUCHEN

8 SERVINGS

Ask an adult to help you make this sweet treat!

INGREDIENTS

1 roll sweet roll dough

4 ounces softened cream cheese

1 large tart apple, sliced

2 teaspoons butter, melted

confectioners' sugar

DIRECTIONS

1. Thaw the sweet roll dough, and spread it in a greased 9 x 13 pan.

2. In a small bowl, combine the cream cheese and sugar. Spread the mixture over the dough.

3. Arrange the apple slices on top and brush them with butter. Cover and let the dough rise in a warm place.

4. Bake at 350 degrees Fahrenheit (177 degrees Celsius) for 25 to 30 minutes or until the crust is golden brown and the apples are tender.

5. Cool on a wire rack. Dust the kuchen with confectioners' sugar. Refrigerate leftovers.

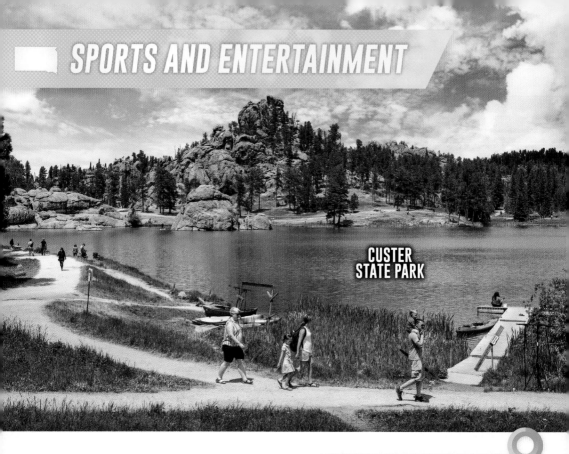

CUSTER
STATE PARK

South Dakotans enjoy the great outdoors. They camp and hike in the state's parks. In summer, swimmers and boaters head to lakes and reservoirs. Winter brings out skiers and snowboarders. Museums attract visitors, too. The Museum of Geology in Rapid City features dinosaur fossils. In Brookings, the South Dakota Art Museum showcases works by the state's artists.

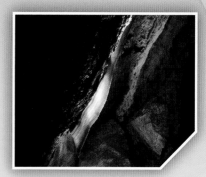

CAVE BACON

Cave explorers have fun at Jewel Cave National Monument in the Black Hills. It features formations called cave bacon. Water flowing over rock for thousands of years created these long, thin sheets of rock that look like bacon.

South Dakotans root for their favorite teams. Baseball fans cheer for the Sioux Falls Canaries. Sioux Falls Stampede games draw ice hockey fans. College sports fans support the University of South Dakota Coyotes.

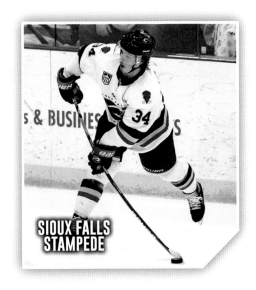

SIOUX FALLS STAMPEDE

NOTABLE SPORTS TEAM

University of South Dakota Coyotes
Sport: NCAA Division 1 women's basketball
Started: 1971
Place of Play: Sanford Coyote Sports Center

STURGIS
MOTORCYCLE RALLY

South Dakota's festivals bring people together. In March, the small town of Freeman celebrates Schmeckfest with traditional German foods. The Sturgis Motorcycle Rally draws big crowds in August. Thousands gather for music, food, and motorcycle rides.

VOLKSMARCH

Volksmarch is a spring and fall tradition at South Dakota's Crazy Horse Memorial. People hike up part of the statue to see the famous Oglala Lakota leader up close.

Custer State Park is home to the Buffalo Roundup and Arts Festival. Every September, crowds watch herders on horseback chase thousands of bison across the prairie. In October, the Black Hills Powwow in Rapid City celebrates Native American traditions with music and dancing. Artists display their work at Winterfest in Aberdeen every November. South Dakotans have a lot to celebrate!

BUFFALO ROUNDUP AND ARTS FESTIVAL

SOUTH DAKOTA TIMELINE

1804
Lewis and Clark arrive at the Missouri River in South Dakota

1700s
Sioux people thrive on the South Dakota plains after pushing out other tribes

1889
South Dakota becomes the 40th state

1803
The United States buys South Dakota from France in the Louisiana Purchase

1874
Gold is discovered in the Black Hills, leading to a gold rush

1903
Wind Cave National Park becomes South Dakota's first national park

1988
Drought leads to a forest fire that destroys 26 square miles (68 square kilometers) of Black Hills forest

1927
Work begins on Mount Rushmore, which is completed in 1941

1890
More than 250 Lakota Sioux lose their lives to the U.S. Army in the Wounded Knee Massacre

2017
More than 200,000 gallons (757,082 liters) of oil spill from the Keystone Pipeline, drawing thousands of protestors

Nickname: The Mount Rushmore State

Motto: Under God, the people rule

Date of Statehood: November 2, 1889 (the 40th state)

Capital City: Pierre ★

Other Major Cities: Sioux Falls, Rapid City, Aberdeen, Brookings, Watertown

Area: 77,116 square miles (199,730 square kilometers); South Dakota is the 17th largest state.

Population

886,667 (2020)

STATE FLAG

South Dakota's flag was adopted in 1992. It is medium blue. Sunrays surround the state seal in the middle. It features a farmer, cattle, a mining operation, and a riverboat. They represent South Dakota's industries. The state name arcs above the seal. The words *The Mount Rushmore State* curve below it.

INDUSTRY

Main Exports

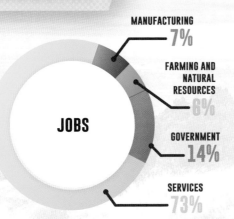

JOBS

MANUFACTURING
7%

FARMING AND NATURAL RESOURCES
6%

GOVERNMENT
14%

SERVICES
73%

soybeans

machinery

animal products

electronic devices

Natural Resources
soil, oil, gold, limestone, granite, gravel

GOVERNMENT

Federal Government
1 REPRESENTATIVE | **2** SENATORS

SD

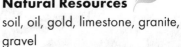

3 ELECTORAL VOTES

USA

State Government
70 REPRESENTATIVES | **35** SENATORS

STATE SYMBOLS

STATE BIRD
RING-NECKED PHEASANT

STATE ANIMAL
COYOTE

STATE FLOWER
AMERICAN PASQUEFLOWER

STATE TREE
BLACK HILLS SPRUCE

GLOSSARY

ancestors—relatives who lived long ago

fry bread—a Native American flatbread made from frying dough

Great Plains—a region of flat or gently rolling land in the central United States

immigrants—people who move to a new country

Louisiana Purchase—a deal made between France and the United States; it gave the United States 828,000 square miles (2,144,510 square kilometers) of land west of the Mississippi River.

pinnacles—high, pointed rocks

powwows—Native American gatherings that usually include dancing

prairie—a large, open area of grassland

replicas—exact copies of things

reservations—areas of land that are controlled by Native American tribes

reservoirs—human-made bodies of water

service jobs—jobs that perform tasks for people or businesses

settlers—people who move to live in a new, undeveloped region

speculators—people who buy land hoping that it will increase in value and will sell for more money later

tourism—the business of people traveling to visit other places

traditional—related to customs, ideas, or beliefs handed down from one generation to the next

Upper Midwest—a region of the United States that includes Minnesota, Wisconsin, Michigan, Iowa, North Dakota, and South Dakota

urban—related to cities and city life

venison—meat from a deer

Wounded Knee Massacre—a conflict between the Lakota Sioux and the U.S. Army; more than 250 Lakota Sioux lost their lives.

TO LEARN MORE

AT THE LIBRARY

Holdren, Annie C. *Building Mount Rushmore*.
Mankato, Minn.: Amicus, 2021.

Kittinger, Jo S. *South Dakota*. New York, N.Y.:
Children's Press, 2019.

Tieck, Sarah. *South Dakota*. Minneapolis, Minn.:
Abdo Publishing, 2020.

ON THE WEB

FACTSURFER

Factsurfer.com gives you
a safe, fun way to find
more information.

1. Go to www.factsurfer.com.

2. Enter "South Dakota" into the search box
   and click 🔍.

3. Select your book cover to see a list
   of related content.

INDEX